praise for
lemon

"Beautiful and Brave" – Megan Falley

"Exploring the sea of our body through poetry, Isabella's book is the beacon for navigational aid. *lemon* encapsulates the time and life of examining one's history and expedition through storytelling." – Masaki Takahashi, Lansing Poet Laureate

"Mansfield's words are honest, sharp, and refreshing. She doesn't sugarcoat the sourness of disability, illness, or trauma, but confronts them head-on with stinging strength. Yes, "the damaged and broken are lemons," and this is a compliment, a rallying cry, because Isabella's poems "spit bitter white pith" right back at you. These poems, filled with emotion and grit, will break your heart, then help you glue the pieces back together."– Kendra Nuttall, author of *A Statistical Study of Randomness*

"In *lemon*, Isabella notes her hospital bracelet identifies her as a "fall risk." True to this warning, the reader experiences the sensation of gradually tumbling downward with her. The poet acts as our patient guide in this process of falling: she ushers us down hospital hallways and into doctors' offices, takes us on a journey across the stars, and moves us through the seasons. Mansfield's collection of poems on disability, ableism, and self-discovery demonstrate an incredible fortitude entirely maintained through a delicate balancing act of attributes gained, lost, and endured."
– Amber Morrison-Fox, Founder and Editor, *Sad Girl Review*

lemon

poems
Isabella J Mansfield

Publisher and Editor:
Isabella J Mansfield – @isabellajmansfield
Howell, MI

Cover Photography
Pete Mundt – @pbmundt

Author Photo
Ryan Rupprecht – @ryan_charles_photography

Graphic Design and Layout
Justin Meister – Rocket Printing @rocketonestop

Press, Author Inquiries, and Booking:
isabellajmansfield@gmail.com

Editing and Proofreading:
Morgan Schlicker, Mary Anna Scenga Kruch, Lena Latham

Additional Typesetting and Editing:
Carrie Shrier and Stevie Pipis

Library of Congress Control Number:
2023901313

poems

Twenty Minutes, Start to Finish

It was finally too cold to rollerblade,
and my brand new skates had been
packed away until spring.
On the carpet in my pajamas,
too close to the television, I sat
eating Oreo cookies for breakfast.
Being a woman of twelve now, *this* was
a decision I felt old enough to make.

But Mom said MTV was
"*too* mature" and blocked it from
the cable lineup, so while my friends
memorized Beavis & Butthead jokes,
I watched Nick at Night, music videos
on VH1, and daydreamed
about being one of the cool kids.

Flamingo legs unfolded
I stretched and danced toward
the kitchen but never made it.
The sudden pain –
wasps don't sting in the house,
in the winter, but something,
somewhere must have attacked
– I did not know it was my own body.

I bent and buckled,
made my way up two stories
now twenty, now thirty,
now the Empire State Building.
My room at the top, reprieve, my bed,
my mother. Certainly there were knives
in my legs, steel, heavy and so cold.
Hands and knees in the carpet now. Just climb.

(continued)

My room right, mother left, bathroom center:
my body would not turn, could not, the tile
cool under my hands and *only* my hands.
I lifted myself, sat, waited. Traced a flat
Laura Ashley pattern under my fingertips. Stood.
The flowers on the wall textured now:
my fingernails ripped the paper, and I fell.

Grief Is a Full Body Experience
    (or *"I spent an entire holiday season in the hospital"*)

that year, the holiday was on fast forward –
time, carried away:
carried down the stairs
carried to the car, into urgent care
carried to the ambulance
to the emergency room
poked and questioned
laid out like dress clothes
palms passing over and over
pressed smooth, picking away
at the invisible, asking
the question "but why?"
grief is not for children
childhood is not
for twelve-year-olds
twelve-year-olds are not adults
adults sit in a conference room
talking about the twelve-year-old
growing stacks of medical records
laid out on an oak table
laid out on a hospital bed
waiting for answers, wasn't invited
to this Christmas party,
wasn't asked how I felt
        only *if* –
if I still felt the chill of December
in my feet, stainless needles
prickling my skin this year instead of pine
IV bag ornaments, sterile tube tinsel
if you listen long enough, the knock
of an MRI could be Jingle Bells
Silent Nights on the sixth floor
of the children's hospital – I wondered

3

(continued)

if the other children still believed,
if they hoped for a Christmas Miracle
if miracles came dressed in white
bearing gifts of relief to drip into the arm
not gripping a teddy bear
those aren't New Year's fireworks
just another new doctor peering lights
into your eyes, looking for answers
waiting to be asked to my first
Valentine's dance instead
of being asked if nerves are still dancing
painfully beneath my skin
naked as a new calendar
waiting for people to stop looking
at me like a mystery to solve
waiting for the adults in the room
to stop talking and take me home

The Damaged and Broken Are Lemons

1.

you hold a paring knife
near every scar
by comparison
as if to measure
each time you were peeled
and sectioned.
this body,
lemon-rind dimpled,
pale as salt where
sugar should be.
sour mouth aching,
you spit bitter white pith.

2.

someone's been playing
Operation and winning
but it is not you. everyone
else has the same pieces,
same instructions, but not you.
you piece together,
with duct tape and old
hospital bracelets,
the broken parts
and find a new way to play
out of necessity.

3.

you are a classified ad
in the bottom of a Penny Saver,
"good value. runs fine."
don't you want to be more than
good and fine? isn't it more
interesting to sputter? cigarette burnt,

(continued)

more missing than broken.
you think you're standing taller
but it is only the cinder blocks.
you are immobile.

4.
if the lemonade is too sour,
it will not be drunk.
if the game loses all the pieces,
it will not be played.
if the car is a lemon,
it will not be moved.

5.
if your body is a lemon –
if it is too damaged
too broken
too diagnosed
too much –
if *you* are too much,
you will not be wanted.

My School Mascot Could Have Been Denial

I returned to East Middle School with four new wheels to carry me: the shiny, new thing, the class distraction. Sixth grade boys scribbled plans, lights and spinners, how to put hydraulics on a wheelchair, make it stand out, though I could no longer stand, and only wanted to disappear. I was known now. Recognized. That Girl. There was no going back to the anonymity of a crowded cafeteria. Everyone knew who I was, but never took the time to know *who I was*. I pulled the worn sleeves of my home, my comfort, my favorite, faded flannel over my hands. Hid beneath the blues and greens of Black Watch plaid and bruises blooming on banged elbows. Developed a thick skin and calloused hands. I learned that sealed lips offered safety. If I wasn't heard, I wasn't seen. If I wasn't seen, I wasn't noticed, and if I wasn't noticed in this new, changed body, maybe I didn't have to notice it, either.

The Space Between My Favorite Season and My Seasonal Depression

At the end of October I drive two hours to wander a sculpture and botanical garden. My doctor and husband both said I needed to relax, to breathe. I pay my admission, pass the gift shop and walk outside. The air is still, clouds mutter maledictions in the distance and I am nearly alone in the cold.

I came here to find… something: inspiration in art or nature, some feeling. Any feeling. I grip the map in my hands until the paper begins to fray. How am I supposed to find myself when these days I can't even find my way out of bed.

A tour passes, and from under her umbrella, the guide describes Rodin's "Eve" as sad. Eve stands there covering her naked, bronze body and hiding her face. Maybe "sad," but I sit behind her and see her fingers clawing her ribcage, as if to pull the covers of her skin back over her body, curl away in anguish and hide and I understand. I pull my jacket closer around my own body and move down the path.

Crack. The silence is broken by black walnuts hitting soft earth. *Crack.* Above me, a squirrel tests the thinner branches at the top. *Crack.* He wants, but is unsure. *Crack.* He decides the reward is not worth the risk, finds another branch to hold him. *Crack.* I put away my pen and empty notebook.

I love the transitional seasons and the way they make me feel like something is coming. This morning the red trees set the horizon on fire, by evening, that fire is extinguished. When I leave the garden, there is no heat left in the ashes.

Doctor's Office, November 12

The doctor prescribes an antidepressant, a low dose; half the children's dose low, just to try it. See if it sticks.

He listens to my symptoms. He laughs in the right moments when I joke as a defense mechanism. He listens to my heart, asks if it races.

I think of the leaves, red and brown ones that raced across the street on my way here.

I tell him "Only when I'm really anxious."

He stops typing, turns back to me. "Do you often have panic attacks?"

"I don't know. Is that what the pounding is?"

I think of the raindrops, fat and heavy on my windshield, maybe a little bit of ice at the edges. He is talking:

"… to take the edge off…"

The edges. Just a little bit.

"… not a bad idea to have this on hand for panic attacks. They'll make you sleepy though." I joke about making sure my panic attacks are only at bedtime. He laughs.

The sky is sleepy gray on the way home. A cold rain had swept through and now, piles of wet leaves stick to cars and roads, sticking to everything but the trees from which they fell.

I think of his words. Just to try it. See if it sticks.

Modern World

Google "how to know if you are suffering
from exhaustion
depression
general malaise"

Google "why do people need each other"
"what is a nervous breakdown"
"how to apologize to your children for yelling
for snapping
for being a bad parent"

Google "how to apologize to your spouse
for not being there
for not being enough"

Hey Siri, what's the weather?
Hey Siri, how long will it rain?
　　　is it ever going to stop
Hey Siri, what time will it be dark?
Hey Siri, can you have a panic attack
　　　only in your head?

Alexa play "sad-day-playlist"
play "rain sounds"
Alexa set a sleep timer for one hour
six hours
forty-seven hours

Google "how to disappear completely"
Google "but not by Radiohead"
Google "how long before you forget someone"

(continued)

Alexa turn off the light
Alexa turn off all notifications
Alexa, help
Alexa… help
Help

Doctor's Office, December 14

From the parking lot, I smell leaves burning somewhere, a heady blend of smoke mixed with nostalgia and a touch of danger. Creatures make their homes here, in the mess of leaves. They function there. They sleep there.

"Let's try increasing your dose up to the baseline. How are you feeling?"

"I'm so tired I can't function. Last week I couldn't stop exercising, all night I kept going, until my body gave out. This week I'm too tired to tie my shoes."

"That sounds like depression. Are you sleeping well?"

I don't tell him that I dream about tornadoes or broken glass or my dead dad.

"Not really."

He asks if I've taken the medication for panic attacks, and I say "One time I needed it but it was 10:30am and I didn't have time for side effects." He tells me to take one tonight and that "there are worse things than a good night's sleep."

In a pile of leaves somewhere, insects have bed down for winter. They sleep too heavily to smell the sulphur of the match.

When It Hits

that tight feeling
in the bottom of
your chest
that fullness
that feeling of
"where do I start"

is this a panic attack?
you don't feel panic
just busy
your to-do list is
one line crossed
three lines added

if only you had more time,
more hours in the day
there is just no way
otherwise to get it done
and failure makes
your chest hurt

the offers to help
are plentiful
even frequent, but god
where do you even start
how can anyone answer when
you can't articulate the question

when it hits, you
keep your head down
keep working, tread water,

(continued)

but make no progress,
walk down the up escalator
watch everyone rise above you

when it hits they will say
"you are depressed again"
but this isn't depressed
or sad or even
anxious, this is just
~~overwhelmed~~ busy
Isn't it?
Isn't it?

this is holding an unbound
book, on a bridge, in
a tornado. Even if you could
find all the pages, you'll
never put them back
together

Bruises

I bruise easier than before.
I don't notice them.
They don't hurt unless
I push them,
which I only do
when they're first discovered:
that unconscious need
to touch
the thing that hurts.

Physician's Order: Fasting Labs

a butterfly
and a plastic
proboscis
drained
five vials
with orders
to uncover
what has made
you sick
but they can't
draw you out
from the
veins beneath
your own skin

Doctor's Office, February 25

"It is just another part," I tell myself.

I joked with the physician's assistant this morning, referring to myself as an empty tin can, thumping my rib cage as she writes down my surgical history. I am not yet aware that this list is about to grow by one.

I let a man take pictures of me with my clothes off. He swore it was just for my chart, and I think "that's a line I haven't heard."

I am tired. Tired in this bed, on this goddamned paper bed, tired of waiting, tired of being here, tired of every part of this body.

"God doesn't make mistakes" but my appendix, my ovaries, uterus, my legs, my spine, my flesh. They don't believe in God anymore.

It would be nice to wear a bracelet that didn't have my name on it, a list of drug allergies and "fall risk." I have been falling for 40 years, every part removed is a little less mass for gravity to pull down.

The man said he needed to consult his colleagues and I think "that's a funny way to say you're showing my nudes around the office." After that, I pulled my clothes on, I went to work. I didn't sit for a moment to consider ~~mourning~~ morning.

It is just another bracelet, another incision, another scar. It is just another part, another mistake. I tell myself I am whole without, but I am too tired to believe it.

They Run Lines

blue ones
in my arms
connect to
clear ones
taped down
plastic snakes
that drip slow
legal
venom

-Ectomy: The Act of Cutting Out

Begin a drip,
quiet the body: breath
aided by machine.

There will be no memory
of a cold, sterile room,
the sounds, the people.

Scalpel glinting,
reflecting blue, peach, red
as small cuts are made.

Separate ligament
from smooth muscle. Extract.
Place on a silver tray for disposal.

Burn the nerves;
one day – not soon,
they will forget the pain.

Close gaping holes.
Leave no visible scars,
only internal ones.

Hollowed Out

I had expected
to feel empty

I had not counted
on feeling so

much in an
empty space

Heat That Comes in Flashes or in Waves

the spring my uterus was removed
started out pleasant, late-April
sweater weather, cloudy days
and we all took for granted
how hot the Arizona summer
was going to be, forgetting
that we live in this arid zone, where
we hide for months in dark tunnels
like the tarantulas we know are beneath
our feet in what once was open desert.

fooled by an incandescent sun
we were lured from our homes,
ambushed by triple-digits, creeping high
as they might be all season with
no buffer between them, no cool desert nights,
when even cactus withers and burns.
When I was sick of myself and my dark tunnel,
I crept out along the sidewalk,
under an empty sky and oppressive sun,
crawling gingerly to warm myself on a rock.

this was a summer everyone felt
for miles, for months, the desert
seeped out of its margins, spread wide
to where it shouldn't have been,
dried and cracked the leaves,
melted asphalt, destroyed fertile
lands and everything felt barren
and empty as desert.
As me.

Transabled
  (or, *Suicide Note from a Leg to a Body*)

In this world exists a group
unnumbered, uncounted,
some sub
        sub
            subculture
who circle the world
for doctors who look
the other way at a code
of ethics, so long as
you have the cash,
to remove healthy limbs
from healthy bodies
disable them permanently
bring them to their knees
        or remove their knees entirely

they disfigure themselves
in the name of idolization,
perhaps fetish or perversion,
some alienation.
They can't shake feeling "wrong;"
to them, a complete body should be
in   com   plete
they long for physical absence
and they'll fight their emptiness
with ropes and tourniquets
with knives
anything to rid themselves
of this flesh without a soul

They want what they don't have,
they don't want what they *do* have,
on some days I worry:

(continued)

My dead-ish limb
still feels, still bleeds
but hangs lifeless,
a shell of what it once was…

What does it say of me
to occasionally wonder:
would it be easier to detach,
to remove dead weight?

would it feel better
to feel nothing at all?

For not wanting what I still have
       but don't have
feeling like a part of my body
doesn't belong, my limb leaves
me waiting for a suicide note it won't write
      a farewell left unsaid
         goodbyes dangling uselessly
                in
           the
              air

Doctor's Office, March 30, April 8, April 24, May 5

"Are you always this complicated?," we laughed, and he said "I'm just kidding," but he wasn't, and he wasn't wrong.

It has been a stormy season.

"I reviewed your MRI. We need to make sure this doesn't get worse," we didn't laugh, he wasn't kidding, and he wasn't wrong.

The May grass has deepened to a rich green with all the rain at its feet.

"I've never seen anything like this, a spine like yours," we laughed, and I said "I think my body was assembled incorrectly." We laugh again. I wasn't kidding.

It would feel more like spring if the sky was less gray, but it has only been gray.

"The good news is, there isn't anything in your results that I would call 'ominous,' but I would like to have you see one of my colleagues in neurosurgery." Nobody laughs.

When I think the sky is clearing, I notice a heavy gray on the horizon. Ominous.

My Naked Body

my naked body
is a work of art

I don't know
if the artist was

Rubens or Dali
or Picasso

I am trying
to find beauty

in it but isn't all
art subjective?

Doctor's Office, May 12

I don't
want to
be here
anymore.

X

I dreamed I woke up
in a different body
one that didn't look inside
like Swiss cheese
wasn't full of scar tissue
one that followed directions

I can't remember which thought
to think to make it move
the way I want
my body is a foreign land
my brain is not from here
it gets lost, gestures crudely
at a shop owner, leaves empty
handed, leaves frustrated
consults a guidebook,
does not understand how
to conjugate verbs
in this language

Have you ever wondered
what the body does inside
when it is missing pieces?
we know muscle will atrophy
I know my bones have twisted
but where there is space
does space fill in? Is there room to stretch
or explore? Does it collapse in on itself?
Are there places you can go
to hear a voice echo where it is empty?

In health class we would study
posters of bodies and learn
"We Are All The Same Inside"

(continued)

but I hang the same poster
and cross off all the pieces
I no longer have
– X marks the spot –
I keep digging for treasure
on this map and soon
the map is full of holes

Maybe I have the wrong map
the wrong island, the wrong body
I could dream myself
to the ends of the earth
searching for uninhabited lands,
uninhibited, but like all
treasure seekers, always looking
to the horizon, but never satisfied
with what they've found

Doctor's Office, May 20

I am on a first name basis with the staff. In every office. They know me before I sign my name at the desk.

Shannon's eyes crinkle at the corners when she laughs, says I am a ray of sunshine, loves when I am in the office.

Patti says Doctor will want me to repeat the ultrasound and have this test done every year. She knows it is uncomfortable, so isn't it nice we have good conversation when I'm on her table?

Rez asks if I finished the poem from my last MRI; when I say I have, he asks if I mentioned "the MRI tech," I did. He grins.

When I enter the next office, someone at the desk says "she's here," and a woman comes from the back, escorts me personally to another office, the neurosurgeon.

We do not speak as we walk down an undecorated hallway. We know this is not the good news walk. We are dismayed to discover the office is closed.

Her name sounds like a moss-covered forest. She says "It's a kind of grape." She is as sweet, but thicker skinned. Grapes do this to protect themselves, too.

She tells me "This doctor is good. It's where I sent my family, that's how you know they're good."

We talk a while in front of the dark office, about poetry, about writing through diagnoses and pain, through shared grief.

They are all so kind, but I don't want to know their names.

(continued)

I don't want them to recognize me, I want to be initials on a chart.
I don't want even *this*.

I don't want to be here. How much can one person handle? My
hands are full, the weight is heavy,

but the printer keeps spilling physician's orders onto the floor
until my feet are covered in paper cuts. There is probably a doctor
for this.

The staff there will greet me as friend, as sunshine, as poem.

Not Everything Is Sacred

my
body
is
a
temple
I
burned
the
temple
to
the
ground

Aisle Nine: Bottled Water, Juice, Clearance, Bible Verses, Unwanted Attention

a man prayed over me
in the clearance aisle
of our neighborhood
grocery store, for my healing
     for the health of
      my broken body
he called me "sister"
said "it isn't enough
to just say the words,
you have to give them power
you have to feel it."

I couldn't tell him
people have laid their hands
on me in every grocery store
from here to Arizona
for the last twenty-nine years
and all it ever did was make me late,
or melt the ice cream

I couldn't tell him
that sure, a miracle would be nice
but I'm not holding my breath
for the day he'll see me turn cartwheels
down that very aisle.

I couldn't tell him
how I'm in the middle of a crisis
of faith, however unrelated
to my "condition," how I feel empty
inside a crowded church
and how I should be bothered
by this but I'm not,

(continued)

because you can't miss something
if you aren't really sure
it was ever there.

Compression

I can't tell you what I am made of,
oxygen, sure, and carbon. I can't tell you
if I am strong. I think I used to be stronger.
I think this version of me is gone.

I suppose she could be out there,
some light years distance. Is she
coming back or rocketing away?
She is too far gone to know.

The images on screen could be
some nebula: gas and dust and
collapsing stars, but it is just my spine,
all white and gray matter. It, too, is collapsing.

The doctor asked when I first noticed
the pain. "which pain," I thought, remembered
that no sound exists in space and from the space
between my lips let slip only "hmm."

Did you know stars
hum themselves
to death in a near
perfect middle C

And I see that he doesn't care I
never noticed the pain. Perhaps I
have adjusted to its gravity, accustomed
to the weight upon my shoulders.

Depression is a weight I have carried,
a constant shifting from one side to another,
always off balance. Stars are born in balance,
gravity compressing to the point of fusion.

(continued)

"This is where the compression occurs,"
he points to my spine. For me, this is where
mental health pushes its way into physical health,
or is it the other way around?

The stronger me must exist in some vast
blue-black of the universe. She could be
discovered, renamed, renumbered.
C5C7-Carbon Star, perhaps. Isabella, less likely.

Primarily oxygen and carbon,
bright and burning. We all imagine
ourselves the central star in our universe,
imagine death in long distance.

My body aches and sinks into itself.
The doctor said it was serious,
then disappeared like a smile.
Serious indeed.

We are born in seconds and die, cell by cell,
in slow motion. Stars are born over a million
years and die in one hundred seconds,
running out of fuel and collapsing.

What the Twelve Year Old Needed to Hear

I know. You feel like your body
is someone else's body, examined
inside and out, machines and eyes
scanning, looking for answers.
Nerves are questions misfired
and stuttering.
Adults fail to explain
words like "neurogenic,"
"inflammation"
and "paralyzed" to your
adolescent understanding.

When I tell you that you
will be okay, I know
you aren't listening. You've
already decided that you are okay,
and this is true, until it isn't:
you will forget picking gravel
from cartwheel-hands,
fresh asphalt and broken-in skates
you will forget the sound of running
        until you don't,
and that is when it hurts most.

Know that it is okay to cry.
Some tears are necessary –
a rock is no less rock
when eroded by tears
or time. You will discover
what you are made of
underneath.

(continued)

From this point, the words
"you can't" will rattle weakening
bones. The word "no" plays
a solemn violin across
atrophied muscle.
Let me be clear: you are no more
burden than bird. You are exactly
the right amount of space.

Your skates will gather dust
in the closet, next to the tap shoes,
the jump rope. Doorways will
widen to ramps you now require
and first dates with doctors
who kiss with needles, instead
of cruel boys who don't know
if they should make eye contact
with you. Disability is not
a skeleton to fear in your closet.

Notice that your shadow
is still your shadow,
even if the body is changed –
time does that, darkness does that,
it is still you in this world.
Do not shrink because someone
does not like the shape of you.

Give yourself permission to exist,
find your voice and use it,
watch them follow your gaze
to the sky, not the earth.

(continued)

When they do not give
access, take it anyway.
One day, when they tell you
"you can't,"
you will tell them

"I already have."

Acknowledgements

Many thanks to the editors and journals who have shared my work with their readers. These poems, or previous versions of them, have been graciously accepted for prior publication:

"The Damaged and Broken Are Lemons" – *Bitchin' Kitsch Winter 2023*

"Grief is a Full Body Experience…" – *Bitchin' Kitsch/All My Relations Vol. 4*

"The Space Between My Favorite Season and My Seasonal Depression" – *Curator Magazine*

"Doctors Office, February 25," "Doctors Office, November 12," and "Doctors Office, December 14," – *Tabula Rasa*

"Transabled – or Suicide Note From a Leg to a Body" – *Disabled Voices Anthology, Rebel Mountain Press*

"Bruises," "They Run Lines," "My Naked Body," and "Aisle Nine…" – *The Hollows of Bone, Finishing Line Press*

Isabella J Mansfield (she/her) writes about anxiety, intimacy, and body image both generally and as a woman with a disability. She has a love for stage poetry, and has taken her work around the country and across the pond, including performances at the Oberon Theater, Cambridge, MA, and Nambucca London. A two-time Pushcart nominee, and a Write Bloody McCarthy Prize Honorable Mention, Isabella is always looking for ways to bring a little humor into her deeply personal poems, and is almost never sorry to make you cry.

Find her on Instagram and Facebook, @isabellajmansfield, and the world's most boring TikTok, @poet_isabella

www.ingramcontent.com/pod-product-compliance
Lightning Source LLC
Chambersburg PA
CBHW070034110426
42741CB00035B/2772